Angus Nicol

NATURAL WORLD

PENGUIN

HABITATS • LIFE CYCLES • FOOD CHAINS • THREATS

Keith Reid

HODDER
Wayland

an imprint of Hodder
Children's Books

WWF

Produced in Association with WWF-UK

NATURAL WORLD

Chimpanzee • Crocodile • Dolphin • Elephant • Giant Panda
Great White Shark • Grizzly Bear • Hippopotamus
Killer Whale • Lion • Orangutan • Penguin • Polar Bear • Tiger

Produced for Hodder Wayland by
Roger Coote Publishing
Gissing's Farm, Fressingfield
Suffolk IP21 5SH, UK

WWF is a registered charity no. 201707
WWF-UK, Panda House, Weyside Park
Godalming, Surrey GU7 1XR

Cover: An adult emperor penguin.
Title page: An emperor penguin in its Antarctic habitat.
Contents page: An adult with its chick.
Index page: An emperor penguin colony.

Editor: Steve Setford
Series editor: Polly Goodman
Designer: Sarah Crouch
Cover designer: Victoria Webb

Published in Great Britain in 2000 by Hodder Wayland,
an imprint of Hodder Children's Books

A Catalogue record for this book is available from the
British Library.

ISBN 0 7502 2692 7

Printed and bound by G. Canale & C. S.p.A. Turin, Italy

Hodder Children's Books
A division of Hodder Headline plc
338 Euston Road, London NW1 3BH

Picture acknowledgements
British Antarctic Survey (Peter Bucktrout) 43; Bryan and
Cherry Alexander 3 (Hans Reinhard), 6, 7, 9, 10, 16 (Hans
Reinhard), 18 (Hans Reinhard), 20 (Hans Reinhard), 22–3
(Steve Pinfield), 28, 29, 30, 33 (Paul Drummond), 34
(Hans Reinhard), 34–5 (Hans Reinhard), 41 (Hans
Reinhard), 42, 44 bottom (Hans Reinhard), 45 top (Hans
Reinhard); Bruce Coleman Collection 15 (Johnny
Johnson), 37 (Johhny Johnson), 44 top (Johnny Johnson),
45 bottom (Johnny Johnson); Digital Stock 8, 18–19, 26,
27, 30–31, 36, 39, 40, 45 middle, 48; FLPA *front cover* (W
Wisniewski); NHPA 21 (Dr Eckart Pott), 24 (Norbert
Wu), 32 (John Shaw), ; Oxford Scientific Films 11 (Doug
Allan), 14 (Doug Allan), 23 (Konrad Wothe), ; Still
Pictures 12 (Thierry Thomas), 13 (Alain Torterotot), 38
(Thierry Thomas), 44 left (Alain Torterotot); Tony Stone
Images 1 (Art Wolfe), 17 (Art Wolfe). Maps on page 4 by
Victoria Webb and Peter Bull. All other artwork by
Michael Posen.

Contents

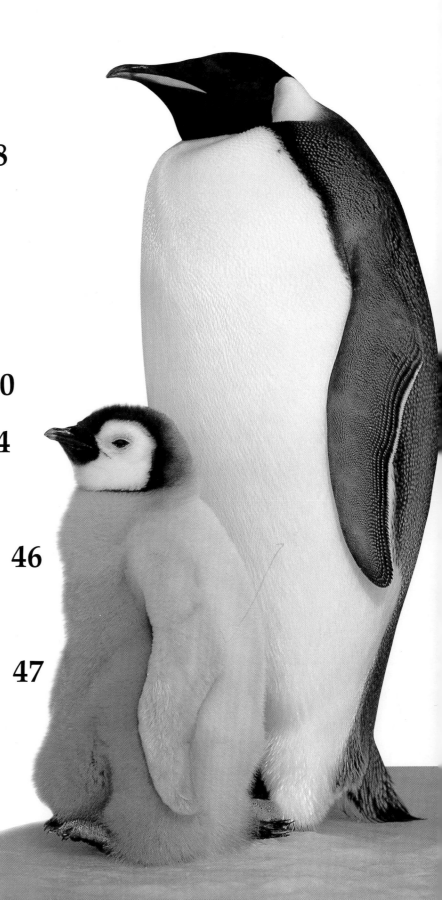

Meet the Penguin

Penguins are flightless seabirds. Their wings have become flippers, which help them swim through water rather than fly through the air. The emperor penguin is the largest of all penguins, and is only found in Antarctica. It is the only species of bird that lays its eggs and raises its chicks during the Antarctic winter, where it faces some of the harshest conditions on Earth.

ANTARCTICA

◀ This map shows Antarctica's position in the world.

South America

ANTARCTICA

South Pole

Australia

New Zealand

▲ On this map of Antarctica, the red shading shows where emperor penguins live. The pink shading shows how far the Antarctic sea-ice extends in winter.

EMPEROR PENGUIN FACTS

The scientific name of the emperor penguin is *Aptenodytes forsteri*. The first part of the name comes from the Greek words meaning 'unwinged diver'. The second part comes from the name of the naturalist J.R. Forster, who visited Antarctica in the 1700s.

●

When fully grown, the emperor penguin stands over 1 metre tall and weighs up to 30 kilograms. Males and females look very similar, and reach similar sizes and weights.

▶ An adult emperor penguin

Nostrils

The nostrils in the penguin's beak are specially adapted for cold weather. They take heat from the penguin's breath as it breathes out, and use this heat to warm the air the penguin takes in with its next breath.

Eyes

The emperor penguin's eyes can see reasonably well – but not excellently – both above and below the water.

Body

The penguin's chunky, streamlined shape enables it to cut though the water with ease.

Flippers

The flippers are the penguin's short, stubby wings, adapted for use in the water. They are stiff and move only at the shoulder, so the penguin cannot fold away its wings like ordinary flying birds. On land, the flippers flap about as the penguin moves around. In the sea, the penguin uses its flippers as paddles, to propel itself through the water.

Feathers

The emperor penguin has a waterproof coat made up of three layers of short, oily feathers. The feathers keep out the water so that the penguin's body stays dry. They also stop the penguin losing vital body heat.

Feet

The feet are set far back on the body, so the penguin walks with a clumsy waddle or a hop. When swimming, the penguin uses its webbed feet as steering rudders, and as brakes to slow down.

Ears

Penguins have good hearing. Their ear openings are covered by feathers and have no outer flaps, like our own.

Blubber

Under the penguin's skin is a thick layer of fat called blubber, which protects the bird from the ice-cold water and freezing wind.

Egg pouch

The emperor penguin has a special pouch-like flap of skin on its belly. The penguin tucks its egg into the pouch, where it can develop in warmth and safety until it is ready to hatch.

The World of the Penguin

There are 17 species of penguin and they all live in the cool waters of the southern hemisphere. One species, the Galapagos penguin, breeds close to the Equator. But it is only found on the Galapagos Islands, off the coast of Ecuador, in South America.

A few species of penguins breed in remote coastal regions of South America, South Africa, Australia and New Zealand. However, the largest numbers of penguins are found in Antarctica and on the small islands around it.

▼ Macaroni penguins are one of six species of penguins that have bright-yellow crest feathers.

The continent of Antarctica is the coldest place on Earth. It covers an area of about 37 million square kilometres, most of it hidden by a sheet of thick ice. At the end of each Antarctic summer, the sea at the edge of the continent begins to freeze and the ice sheet grows, so that the area of the Antarctic almost doubles.

At the end of the winter, the sea-ice melts and gradually shrinks back to the edges of the continent. The advance and retreat of the sea-ice happens each year. This book will tell you about the life of the emperor penguin on the Antarctic sea-ice.

▲ Icebergs come in a range of shapes and colours – even blue! Penguins, like these chinstrap and gentoo penguins, are often seen sitting on them.

From Egg to Chick

It is May, at the beginning of the Antarctic winter. Pairs of adult male and female emperor penguins are gathered in large groups, called colonies, on the frozen sea-ice. There are less than 50 colonies of emperor penguins in Antarctica. Some colonies are small, although there are five colonies with more than 20,000 birds. The largest colony contains as many as 25,000 penguins.

▲ Emperor penguins gather on the frozen sea-ice to breed.

The female emperor penguin lays a single, greenish-white egg. The egg is about 12 centimetres long, 8 centimetres wide and weighs about 400 grams. Emperor penguins do not build nests, so the female penguin lays the egg directly on to her own feet.

▲ A scientist measuring the egg of an emperor penguin.

Passing the Egg

Shortly after the egg has been laid, the female passes it to the male, who has been waiting to take over the duties of incubating the egg. The male quickly rolls the egg on to his feet and covers it with a special fold of skin. This fold forms a pouch for the egg and protects it from the icy conditions.

The moment when the egg passes from the female to the male is a very dangerous time. If the egg touches the ice for more than a few seconds, the intense cold may cause it to crack, and then it will never hatch. Should anything happen to this egg, it will be a whole year before the female is able to lay another one.

▲ After laying the egg, the female penguins leave the colony and head off to the sea to feed.

As soon as the female has safely passed the egg to the male, she leaves him and goes to sea to feed. She will return in early July, when the egg is ready to hatch.

◀ With the egg now safely in his pouch, the male stays behind in the colony to incubate the egg until it hatches.

▲ Penguins face some of the coldest conditions on Earth during the Antarctic winter.

Incubating in the Dark

By June, the middle of the Antarctic winter, temperatures may drop to -40 °C. It feels even colder because of the wind-chill, produced by winds blowing at up to 200 kilometres per hour.

At this time of year, the sun never rises above the horizon. It is dark and very cold for 24 hours a day. The male penguin relies on his dense covering of feathers and a thick layer of blubber to help keep him warm.

ENERGY FROM BLUBBER

By midwinter, it will be nearly 100 days since the male penguin last fed. He gets the energy he needs to survive by using up fat stored in a layer of blubber under his skin. The fat is broken down into sugary substances, which provide the energy to keep the penguin's body working.

12

During the worst conditions, when the freezing wind is at its strongest, the males huddle together in large groups for warmth. As many as 5,000 penguins pack tightly together. The temperature at the centre of the huddle may be 10 °C warmer than outside.

Penguins on the side of the huddle that is exposed to the wind gradually move towards the middle of the group. Other penguins take their place on the outside. By all moving in this way, the penguins make sure that each one spends the same amount of time in the warmest part of the huddle.

▼ In the very coldest conditions, large groups of male penguins huddle together to keep warm.

The Eggs Hatch

By early July, the egg is almost ready to hatch in the warmth of the male's pouch. The temperature in the pouch may be as much as 70 °C warmer than the air outside. Most of the eggs in the colony hatch within a few days of each other, and this is a time of great excitement amongst the penguins.

▼ These two-week-old chicks are held above the cold ice and snow on their parents' feet.

Soon after the egg hatches, the male emperor feeds the chick. Even though he has not eaten since March, he is still able to bring up food from his stomach and pass a small meal to the chick, from beak to beak. The chick weighs about 300 grams.

The female emperor penguins come back to the colony when the eggs are hatching. Despite having been away for two months, they somehow know when the eggs are due to hatch. They start to arrive back at the colony within a day of the chick first appearing. The males welcome their partners back with a special trumpeting call.

▲ Very young chicks must be careful to stay in the warmth of their parent's pouch.

Growing Up

▼ Moving between parents can be a dangerous time for small chicks.

Now that the female has returned to the colony, she is able to feed the chick with food she has brought back from the sea. Before its mother can feed it, the chick must swap from its father's incubation pouch to a similar pouch on its mother. This is one of the most dangerous moments in a chick's early life. If it stays on the ice for more than a few moments, it may freeze to death.

Occasionally, an adult penguin whose own chick has died will try to steal another chick that it sees out on the ice. It does this by rushing up to the unattended chick and pushing it into its own incubation pouch with its beak. But without the special bond that exists between a parent and its own chick, the foster parent will eventually abandon the chick and it will die.

The risk of freezing to death or being stolen by another penguin means that the chick passes quickly from its father to its mother.

▶ An emperor penguin chick with its parents.

Back to the Sea

With the chick now safely in the female's pouch, the male can make the long journey to the sea to feed. Since it is winter, the sea-ice is at its greatest extent, so the open sea may be as much as 100 kilometres away. The journey can take the male up to a week of walking and tobogganing. Tobogganing is when a penguin lies on its belly and pushes itself along with its flippers and feet.

▼ Sliding along on its belly, called tobogganing, is an easy way for a penguin to travel over smooth snow and ice.

▲ The long walk to the open sea, where the penguins can feed, may take several days.

Once the male reaches the sea he can begin feeding, to put back the weight he has lost while incubating the egg. He returns to the colony with food for the chick after about three weeks. He then looks after the chick while the female takes her turn to go back to sea to feed.

Nursery Groups

When it is about a month old, the chick is big enough to make brief trips out on to the ice to explore its frozen home. It must be careful to stay close to its mother or father, because the weather can change for the worse very quickly.

▼ Groups of chicks huddle together in a crèche to keep warm.

At three months, the chick weighs about
2 kilograms. It is now big enough to leave its
parents' protection altogether and join other
chicks in a big group called a crèche, which is
rather like a penguin nursery. In each crèche, large
numbers of chicks huddle together for warmth,
just like the males did earlier in the winter.

Fortunately, emperor penguin colonies are in such
remote, hostile places that there is usually little
risk of chicks falling prey to predators.

▲ Some chicks fall
victim to the freezing
weather and do not
survive the winter.

The End of Winter

By September, the worst of the winter has passed and the days get lighter every day. Once the chick is old enough to be left in the crèche, both parents can travel across the sea-ice to feed and bring back food.

As the weather gets warmer, the sea-ice melts and starts to retreat, so that the adults' journey to and from the open sea gets shorter. This means that the parents are able to bring food back to the chick more often, and the chick grows rapidly.

▲ Parents leave the colony to bring back food for their chicks.

If the retreat of the sea-ice is too slow, the parent birds have too far to travel and cannot bring enough food back to their chick, leading to starvation. On the other hand, if the sea-ice breaks up too quickly, chicks may fall into the water before they have grown their waterproof feathers, risking drowning or freezing to death.

▶ Food is passed directly from beak to beak when the parent returns.

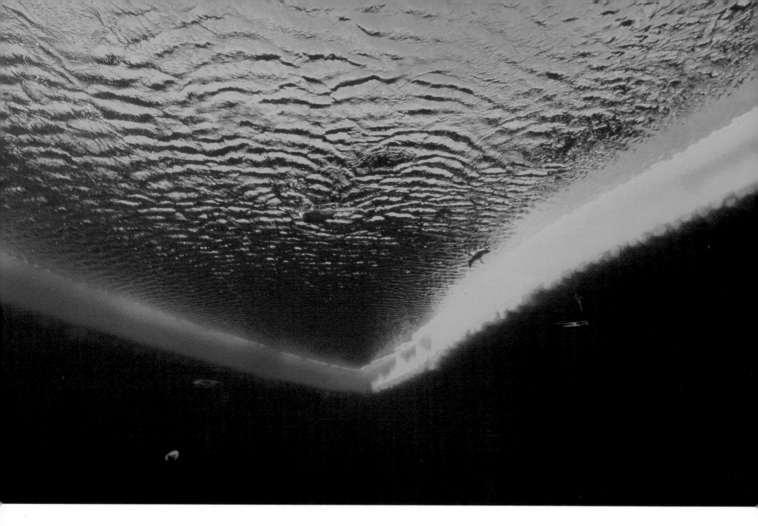

▲ This photograph was taken underwater looking up towards the surface. You can see the sea-ice and an emperor penguin about to dive.

Food and Feeding

Penguins feed by diving to catch small, shrimp-like creatures called krill, as well as fish and small squid. They are excellent divers and usually dive to depths of between 50 and 100 metres. They can stay underwater for 2–3 minutes. The deepest dives reach an incredible 500 metres and last up to 20 minutes.

Sometimes emperor penguins feed close to the sea-bed, although the depth to which they will dive depends on the type of food they are looking for. On a feeding trip an adult emperor penguin may make as many as 100 dives in a single day.

PENGUIN FOOD CHAIN

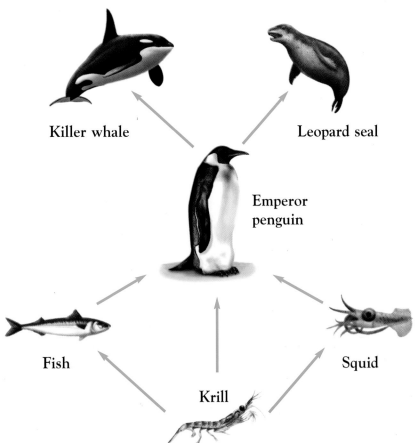

Killer whale

Leopard seal

Emperor penguin

As well as finding enough food for themselves, the parent penguins must bring back larger and larger amounts to the colony to feed their ever-hungry chicks. Each parent can bring back over 1 kilogram of food on each visit to the colony.

Fish

Squid

Krill

Phytoplankton

ANTARCTIC KRILL

Krill are at the centre of the Antarctic food-web. Krill feed on microscopic plants called phytoplankton, which use the energy in sunlight to make food for themselves. Krill, in turn, are eaten by whales, seals, other penguins and sea birds in the Antarctic. Although most of us will never see one, Antarctic krill are among the most numerous living things on Earth.

▲ Emperor penguins feed mainly on krill, fish and small squid.

Finding the Chick

As the chick grows, it needs lots of food, both to grow and to keep itself warm. The two parents are kept busy bringing a constant supply of food back to the chick.

A large colony of emperor penguins may contain several thousand chicks who all look very similar and are all very hungry. Because of this, it is vital that the two parents can easily find their own chick when they return to the colony.

▲ This chick sits head upwards and calls to its parents so that they can deliver its food.

As the parents approach the colony, they give a unique call that the chick can recognize. The chick replies with a unique call of its own. Parents and chicks will keep calling until they meet each other. Even though the colony is a crowded, noisy place, the emperor penguin parents always find their chick.

▲ Being able to recognize each other is important for both adults and chicks in such large colonies.

27

Time to Leave

At the age of five months, the penguin chick weighs around 15 kilograms – about thirty times more than when it was born. At this time, its parents stop returning with food for it and the chick knows that it must go to the sea to find food for itself.

▲ These large chicks are almost ready to lose their down – their chick feathers – and begin to moult.

Before it can go to the sea, the chick must moult. This means that it loses its downy feathers and gains a new, streamlined coat of waterproof feathers, just like its parents.

The first chicks to leave the colony and head for the sea follow adult penguins that are still making the journey to feed younger chicks. The young penguins make their way to the edge of the ice, where they catch their first-ever glimpse of the open sea.

▼ Chicks begin to moult the down from their bellies first. Soon they will look as smooth as their parents.

To the Sea

The young penguins first enter the sea in December, the middle of the Antarctic summer, when food is at its most plentiful. The young are only about half the size of their parents, so it is very important that they are able to find lots of food to help them to grow to full size quickly.

By breeding and rearing their chick on the ice during winter, the adult emperor penguins ensure that the chick enters the sea at the time of year when the water is teeming with life and food is easiest to find. At any other time of year, the chick would starve.

▼ As soon as they are ready, small groups of chicks make their way to the edge of the sea.

▶ Emperor penguins dive into the sea from the edge of the ice. The temperature above the ice may be as low as –20 °C, but the sea never gets lower than –2 °C.

Life in the Water

When the chicks first take to the water, they enter a completely new environment. The sea is only a few degrees above freezing and there are lots of icebergs of all different shapes and sizes – some up to 100 kilometres long.

Even though the young penguins have never even seen the sea before, they are able to swim and dive straight away. They must learn quickly how to catch food, without their parents there to teach them.

Scientists know very little about what happens to these young penguins once they enter the sea. However, young emperor penguins have been known to travel up to 2,000 kilometres from the Antarctic within their first month in the water.

▲ The leopard seal has powerful jaws and sometimes eats penguins.

▶ Weddel seals spend much of their time under the ice, where they feed on krill and fish.

A NEW WORLD

The young penguins see many new sights in their watery world, including weddel seals, minke whales and crab-eater seals (which do not actually eat crabs, but feed on Antarctic krill). The Antarctic sea is also home to Adélie penguins, which are much smaller than the emperors.

Adult Life

For the first five years of its life, the young emperor penguin spends all of its time in the sea, or on icebergs. At the age of five, it returns to the colony in which it was born to find a mate and raise a chick of its own.

◀ As they return to breed, emperor penguins leap out of the water on to the sea-ice.

At the end of March, as the sea begins to freeze over again, most animals and birds leave the Antarctic for warmer places, to avoid the harsh Antarctic winter. However, this is the time when emperor penguins jump out of the sea on to the ice and begin their long walk to their breeding colonies.

▲ A long line of emperor penguins make their way back to their colonies to begin breeding.

FINDING THE WAY

Emperor penguin colonies are in the same place each year, but it is a mystery how the young adults find their way back to the colony they left five years ago. Getting to the colonies involves a long walk across a featureless landscape, without any distinctive landmarks to help the penguins find their way. Scientists are puzzled as to how they can do this.

Finding a Mate

As soon as the penguins arrive at the colony, they find a mate by performing a special courtship display. A male penguin gives a series of trumpeting calls. If a female is interested in him, she replies with a call of her own.

▲ A male and female emperor penguin form a special bond to help them raise their chick.

◀ Somehow emperor penguins manage to find their colonies even though there are no obvious landmarks to guide them.

The pair stand face to face, calling to each other with their bills pointing down towards their feet.

When the pair have decided that they are happy with each other, the female follows the male around the colony in a special waddling walk. Once they have mated, both the male and female will stay together in the colony for about 45 days until the new egg is laid.

Lifespan

Although they inhabit such a harsh environment, emperor penguins can live for as long as twenty years. After returning to breed for the first time at five years old, they breed every year.

Illness and disease do not seem to affect emperor penguins too greatly. But because of the harshness of their environment, only the fit and healthy survive – penguins that grow infirm with age soon perish.

▲ Some of these chicks may grow up to spend fifteen winters in the Antarctic rearing chicks of their own.

Predators

Although emperor penguins are not threatened by land predators, there are still dangers at sea from marine mammals such as killer whales or leopard seals. Both of these predators are often seen trying to catch unwary emperor penguins along the edge of the ice, especially near the places where the penguins enter and leave the sea.

▼ Killer whales hunt at the edge of the sea-ice, where penguins enter the water. These two are looking across the ice, trying to spot penguins coming their way.

Risks and Threats

The lives of emperor penguins are ruled by the sea-ice, so any major change to their environment could be a threat to them.

Using special satellites, scientists are able to record differences in the amount of sea-ice around Antarctica from year to year. Some studies suggest that global warming may be causing changes in the pattern of sea-ice, which could have a harmful effect on the penguins.

▼ Aerial photographs and satellite pictures of the Antarctic show changes in the position of the edge of the sea-ice.

The Antarctic Treaty is an agreement designed to ensure that Antarctica is kept as a peaceful place and only used for scientific research. The treaty was originally signed in June 1961 by twelve countries, and has now been signed by another forty-three. Under the treaty, no one is allowed to bring plants or animals into Antarctica that could introduce diseases.

▲ All antarctic wildlife, including emperor penguins, are protected by the Antarctic Treaty.

The Commission for the Conservation of Antarctic Marine Living Resources was set up in 1980 under the Antarctic Treaty to make sure that fishing around Antarctica does not affect the delicate balance of Antarctic wildlife. This should make sure that fishing vessels do not catch too much krill, which are so important to marine life in Antarctic waters.

Pollution

Tourism is increasing in Antarctica, but because it takes place during the summer months (November to February) it is unlikely to cause too much disturbance to breeding emperor penguins. Even so, it is important that all tourism is very carefully controlled to make sure that tourists do not spoil the very special nature of Antarctica.

There is a small number of scientific research bases in Antarctica, and under the Antarctic Treaty they must all remove their waste so that it cannot pollute the environment.

▲ Tourists must follow strict rules to avoid disturbing these penguin chicks.

Pollution levels are low in the Antarctic, but pollution elsewhere in the world creates a huge hole in the ozone layer above Antarctica each year. The ozone layer is the layer of ozone gas in the atmosphere that protects animals and plants from the damaging ultraviolet rays. So if we work hard to create less pollution, the future of emperor penguins far away in Antarctica will be much safer.

You can find details of some of the organizations trying to help emperor penguins and protect the Antarctic environment on page 47.

▼ A scientific research base in Antarctica.

Emperor Penguin Life Cycle

 **1** Emperor penguins breed in colonies on the Antarctic ice at the beginning of the winter, perhaps 100 kilometres from the sea. The female penguin lays a single egg. She passes the egg to the male and then sets off for the sea.

 **2** The male keeps the egg in a special pouch until it is ready to hatch. To survive the harsh winter weather and protect their eggs, the male penguins in the colony huddle together with others for warmth.

 **3** The female returns from the sea when the egg hatches. She is greeted by a loud trumpeting call from the male. The female now looks after the chick and the male goes off to sea to feed for the first time in many months.

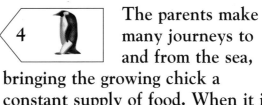

4 The parents make many journeys to and from the sea, bringing the growing chick a constant supply of food. When it is big enough, the chick joins a huddle of other chicks, called a crèche.

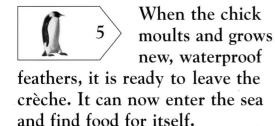

5 When the chick moults and grows new, waterproof feathers, it is ready to leave the crèche. It can now enter the sea and find food for itself.

6 After five years, the young penguins return to the breeding colony to find a mate and raise a chick of their own.

GEOGRAPHY
- Mapwork: where penguins live.
- Environmental change: ozone layer, global warming and reduction of sea-ice
- Ecotourism: penguin-watching
- Food journeys

ART
- Camouflage
- Shape and movement
- Water in art

SCIENCE
- Ocean habitat
- Classification: flightless birds
- Heat and warmth: body fat
- Adaptation: penguin's body shape
- Penguin's life cycle
- Food chains and pollution
- Protection of the marine environment

Penguin Topic Web

MATHS
- Penguin numbers
- Height and weight comparisons
- Compare the energy value of different prey

ICT
- Conservation groups' websites
- Write an email to a zoo, expressing a point of view

ENGLISH
- Origins of names: scientific and common

Extension Activities

English
- Debate the theme 'should penguins be kept in zoos?'
- Find and list collective names for groups of animals, or terms for their young, e.g. chick, pup, cub.
- Write a letter to a conservation group expressing a point of view.

Geography
- Trace a world map from an atlas. Show the location of Antarctica.
- Draw a map showing Antarctica close-up, on a different scale.
- Draw a penguin distribution map.

Science
- Make a chart showing how parts of the penguin's body are specially adapted for certain functions.
- Discuss the effect of global warming on the penguin and other polar animals.
- Compare the way penguins and humans raise their young. What are the similarities and differences?
- List the similarities and differences between a penguin and a sparrow.

Dance and Drama
- Make up a dance that shows a young penguin shuffling and tobogganing to the sea.

Glossary

Colony A large group of animals which live together to mate and raise young.

Courtship The behaviour of an animal that leads to mating.

Crèche A group of young penguins that huddle together for warmth.

Egg pouch A pocket on the emperor penguin's belly made by a special fold of skin. It covers the egg, which the penguin keeps on top of its feet.

Food chain The way animals and plants depend on each other for food.

Global warming The gradual increase in the temperature of the Earth caused by pollution in the atmosphere.

Icebergs Large pieces of ice that have broken off the Antarctic ice sheet.

Incubating Keeping an egg warm so that the chick can develop properly inside.

Krill Shrimp-like creatures in the ocean.

Moult To replace old feathers with new ones. Many birds moult gradually, but penguins replace all their feathers at once.

Phytoplankton Microscopic plants that live in the ocean and use the energy in sunlight to make food.

Pollution The spoiling of the environment by dumping chemicals and waste on land and at sea, and releasing harmful gases into the atmosphere.

Research base Specially designed buildings used by scientists to live and work all year round in Antarctica.

Ozone layer A thin layer of ozone gas in the atmosphere, which filters out the sun's harmful ultraviolet rays.

Streamlined Having a smooth shape that moves easily through air or water.

Wind-chill When the temperature feels lower than it really is because of the wind.

Further Information

Organisations to Contact

WWF-UK
Panda House, Weyside Park,
Godalming, Surrey GU7 1XR
Tel 01483 426444
Website: www.wwf-uk.org

British Antarctic Survey,
High Cross, Madingley Road,
Cambridge CB30ET
Tel. 01223 361188

Websites

http://www.nerc-bas.ac.uk/
public/schools/schools.html
Information for schools from
the British Antarctic Survey.

http://www.seaworld.org/
Penguins/pageone.html
In-depth information on
penguin biology and lifestyle.

Books to Read

Antarctic Wildlife by Ben
Osborne (Oxford Scientific
Films, 1989)
Arctic and Antarctic by Barbara
Taylor (Dorling Kindersley
Eyewitness guides, 1995)
*Playing with Penguins and Other
Adventures in Antarctica* by Ann
McGovern and Colin Monteath
(Scholastic, 1994)

Index

All the numbers in **bold** refer to photographs or illustrations.